Original title:
Groves of Giggles

Copyright © 2025 Creative Arts Management OÜ
All rights reserved.

Author: Theodore Sinclair
ISBN HARDBACK: 978-1-80567-422-1
ISBN PAPERBACK: 978-1-80567-721-5

The Color of Cheerfulness

In a land where laughter blooms,
Colors burst like big balloons,
Yellow ducks in purple hats,
Waddle by with silly chats.

Jellybeans fall from the trees,
Tickling noses with a breeze,
Rainbows hide in cotton clouds,
Chasing giggles in big crowds.

Silly Shadows Dancing

Shadows stretch and twist around,
Doing jigs upon the ground,
Silly hats atop their heads,
Jiving joy from flower beds.

Lampshades bounce, they leap and swirl,
A canvas where the giggles whirl,
Every corner gleams with cheer,
As shadows laugh, we gather near.

The Meadow's Merriment

In a meadow bright and wide,
Bouncing bunnies jump with pride,
Daisies dance, the wind's delight,
Each petal twirls in pure delight.

Squirrels prance with comic flair,
Chasing tails through fragrant air,
Laughter leaps from bloom to bloom,
Filling up the sunny room.

Exuberance Among the Oaks

Under oaks where giggles rise,
Silly squirrels plot the skies,
Wiggling branches tell a joke,
Each leaf whispers, laughter's cloak.

Pinecones drop like little balls,
Rolling down as fun befalls,
With each plop, the chuckles grow,
A merry dance in nature's show.

The Rhythm of Raucous Revelry

In the woods where laughter flows,
Mice wear shoes, and the parrot knows.
Squirrels dance on banana peels,
While the raccoon spins and squeals.

Frogs juggle bugs, what a sight!
Owls have a talent show at night.
The trees shimmy, the flowers cheer,
As clowns parade full of good cheer.

Jumping jacks with the hedgehog crew,
With silly hats and a wacky brew.
Turtles race in a comical way,
While the shadows in the moonlight sway.

Laughter echoes through the air,
Hiccups burst from a badger's lair.
When the sun goes down and stars appear,
The woodland revelry brings good cheer.

Fanciful Fables of the Forest

In a glen where giggles bloom,
Bunnies hop in a velvet room.
With tea parties on toadstool chairs,
And gossip shared in curious stares.

Tales of ducks who tap dance bright,
And bees who play tag before the night.
A hedgehog dressed as a dapper gent,
Charmed the fox with his wise content.

Chasing shadows, the fox took flight,
Over hills, with a jest so light.
They laughed till dawn kissed the trees,
As the breeze carried their joyous pleas.

Every leaf held a secret tune,
While the moon winks, a cheeky boon.
In this world of wild delight,
Each moment wrapped in purest light.

Serenade of the Sprightly

In a field where laughter flows,
Each step is dance, and joy bestows.
Silly hats upon our heads,
As giggles bounce on feather beds.

Chasing shadows, quick and bright,
Tickled toes in warm daylight.
We spin like tops, no care in sight,
With frolic lights that chase the night.

Mirthful Melodies in the Mist

Whispers in the morning haze,
Giggling frogs in merry ways.
Swaying branches, playful tunes,
Bouncing bubbles, laughing moons.

In puddles deep, we splash around,
Our silly voices, joyous sound.
Misty giggles fill the air,
With every hop, we show we care.

Joyous Journeys Through the Underbrush

Adventurers on a merry quest,
Finding critters, nature's jest.
Squirrels jive, as we rejoice,
In every rustle, hear the voice.

We stumble, trip, and laugh so loud,
Each tumble brings a playful crowd.
With every twist upon the trail,
Our giggles echo, never pale.

Giddy Gatherings in the Glade

Under branches swaying wide,
We gather 'round, our hearts are tied.
With every story, laughter grows,
As friendship blooms like springtime's rose.

Cupcakes, sprinkles, joy to share,
A dance around, a silly flare.
In the glade, we spin and whirl,
A tapestry of giggles swirl.

The Mischievous Thicket

In the thicket, shadows play,
Where the critters joke all day.
A squirrel's prank, a rabbit's cheer,
They tumble down, without a fear.

The trees sway, a giggling band,
Each branch holds laughter, unplanned.
A bumblebee hums silly tunes,
While dandelions dance like loons.

In this realm, the laughter grows,
With every rustle, mischief flows.
A butterfly in a silly spin,
Racing the breeze to join the din.

Ah, the fun that flora lends,
With nature's sprites, life never ends.
A chatty crow, a hopping mouse,
Create a joy like none other house.

Frolicsome Voices in the Breeze

Whispers tickle in the air,
As sunbeams dance without a care.
Leaves chuckle in the gentle sway,
Sharing secrets of the day.

A jaybird sings a silly tune,
While flowers sway beneath the moon.
The breeze carries laughter far,
Like twinkling tunes from a ukulele guitar.

In this place, glee never tires,
As nature sparks joyful fires.
The sunbeam's kiss, a prankster's light,
Turns ordinary into pure delight.

Every rustle hides a tease,
Laughter tumbles through the trees.
In the whispers, life's a game,
Joyful hearts, never the same.

Sprightly Sagas of the Outdoors

Under the sky, tales unfold,
Of playful critters, brave and bold.
The breeze carries a story tight,
Of acorns flying, what a sight!

A turtle tells a silly plot,
Of racing snails, believe it or not.
Each squirrel boasts of leaps so wide,
While cheeky mice find joy in pride.

The woodland plays a lively tune,
As shadows dance beneath the moon.
With every hop, a cheer, a laugh,
Nature's joke, a perfect gaffe.

Around the bend, a prankster's call,
Echoes sweetly, inviting all.
In this saga, giggles reign,
As sunshine drapes the grassy plain.

Laughter's Leafy Retreat

In a leafy nook, laughter stirs,
Bubbly giggles, chittering furs.
A raccoon hides, plotting a jest,
As playful winds give nature rest.

Tiny fairies whisper and tease,
Twirling about with grace and ease.
Sunshine drips like honey's glow,
Creating mischief as they go.

Every branch becomes a stage,
In this retreat, they laugh and engage.
A funny tale, a tale so sweet,
Where echoes of joy are hard to beat.

As sunset paints the sky with cheer,
The forest finds its laughter clear.
From every leaf, a chuckle bursts,
In this haven where glee converses.

The Secret of Chucklewood

In the realm where laughter grows, A tickle from a wiggly nose. Trees wear jests, dressed up in glee, Whispers echo, 'Come laugh with me!'

Branches sway with playful tunes, Napping squirrels wear silly loons. The breeze hums jokes both wild and free, Fungi giggle, 'Just wait and see!'

A hidden path of jolly pranks, Where every shadow giggles, thanks! Butterflies in costumes bloom, They flutter here, dispelling gloom.

So wander deep where smiles ignite, In Chucklewood, pure delight. With every step, a chuckle's found, The secret's joy, forever bound.

Mirth Beneath the Leaves

Beneath the branches, mirth resides, Where silly wisdom oft abides. A cat in socks climbs up a tree, A quirky sight, so wild and free!

Twirling ferns with giggly grins, Tap-dancing ants in tattered fins. The sunbeams chase the shadows wide, As laughter echoes, side by side.

Owls wear glasses, wise and bright, They crack the jokes that cause delight. As crows compete in feathered wear, The woods erupt in joyful flare.

In this place where fun takes flight, Mirth beneath the leaves shines bright. A world where every heart can sing, Embrace the joy that nature brings!

Treetop Hijinks

Up in the branches, mischief thrives, Where monkeys swing and humor jives. Squirrels play pranks in leafy halls, Each giggle bounces off the walls.

A raccoon wears a shiny hat, As laughter rings from here to that. The parrot squawks a silly rhyme, A clock that ticks—just wasting time!

With apples tossed in playful fights, The critters dance on vibrant lights. A jester's crown on every head, In treetop hijinks, joy is spread.

So climb the ladders of pure fun, Handstands under the golden sun. Here in the tops, where spirits soar, The laughter echoes, evermore!

Sunlight and Snickers

Sunlit glades where giggles play, Each beam of light a bright bouquet. Laughter weaves through leaves with grace, As nature wears a funny face.

Dandelions wear crown-like hats, While beetles dance with acrobats. The brook babbles a snickering tune, Under the watch of a cheeky moon.

Wind whispers jokes among the trees, Tickling softly, as it flees. A friendly breeze that twirls around, Spreading joy without a sound.

So settle in this vibrant nook, With sunlight and snickers, take a look. Embrace the warmth of every cheer, Let laughter's echo be your steer!

Panoply of Playful Whispers

In the shady nooks they giggle,
Silly sounds that make you wiggle.
Laughter dances on the breeze,
As the flowers sway with ease.

Bouncing balls and tickled toes,
Where the playful spirit grows.
Round the corners, peek-a-boo,
Laughter brightens skies so blue.

The Jolly Trail of Ticklish Trees

Down the path of chuckles sweet,
Trees with faces, quite a feat!
Branches wave in gentle glee,
Whispering tales to you and me.

Squirrels dance and birds all croon,
Underneath the gleeful moon.
Rustling leaves share secret laughs,
As we stroll on playful paths.

Harmonies of Happiness in the Thicket

In the thicket, joy takes flight,
With each giggle, hearts feel light.
Sunbeams tickle, shadows play,
Laughter brightens up the day.

Caterpillars do the twist,
In this merry, funny tryst.
Frogs in chorus, join the cheer,
As joy spills out year by year.

The Frost of Fun in the Glade

In the glade where giggles freeze,
Snowflakes twirl like happy keys.
Winter's chill, a playful friend,
Crafting joy that knows no end.

Snowmen wink with carrot smiles,
Sledding down the snowy piles.
Whirl and twirl, the fun won't cease,
In this frosty place of peace.

Merry Mischief in the Woodland

In the thicket, laughter sings,
Squirrels dance on springy springs.
Berries wobble, giggles roll,
Nuts and jokes, they take a stroll.

Beneath the boughs, a ticklish breeze,
Bumblebees buzz with playful ease.
A rabbit hops, a prankster bold,
Telling tales of mischief gold.

Chipmunks chime in, a cheeky crew,
Swinging from branches, oh what a view!
The forest floor, a playful site,
Where even shadows join the light.

With each rustle, a joke to share,
Leaves burst forth in jovial flair.
Nature's jesters, full of cheer,
A woodland party, draw near, draw near!

Enigmatic Euphoria of the Evergreens

Tall and twisty, the trees conspire,
Whispers float, they never tire.
Laughter echoes, a riddle spun,
Where glimmers of joy outshine the sun.

Pinecones tumble with a clatter,
Each sound a giggle, a merry matter.
With every rustle, secrets pass,
The branches sway, in a dance so brash.

Hidden nooks of joyful glee,
Where fairy tales hide, wild and free.
A dash of whimsy, a sprinkle of fun,
An exuberant race, till the day is done.

Mirthful laughter fills the air,
Enigmas swirl, without a care.
In this haven, trouble seems light,
Where the trees wear smiles, oh what a sight!

Whispers of Laughter

In a glade where giggles bloom,
Softly rippling, joy assumes.
Crickets chirp a silly song,
While creatures laugh the whole day long.

The wind carries secrets on its wings,
Ticklish moments that nature brings.
Breezes tease, they twist and play,
With every gust, they call "Hooray!"

Raccoons peek from behind the trees,
Poking fun as they aim to please.
Echoes of chuckles twirl and weave,
In this realm, who'd dare to leave?

Joyful whispers, a playful delight,
Laughter swirls under the moonlight.
In the hush of night, giggles take flight,
Creating dreams with pure delight.

Echoes in the Canopy

Underneath the leafy dome,
The world is bright, a laughter's home.
Chirpy birds with witty calls,
Share their jokes over leafy halls.

Amidst the branches, a splashing sound,
A squirrel's leap, from round to round.
Old owls chuckle, wise and sly,
With glinting eyes, they survey the sky.

Each rustling leaf, a giggle flies,
Shadows dance, where whimsy lies.
Nuts roll down, pranksters in play,
Nature's comedy, unfolding ballet.

Laughter echoes, a vibrant tune,
Mischievous whispers beneath the moon.
Brighten your step, let joy expand,
For in this haven, together we stand!

Quirky Conversations Under the Canopy

In the shade, the squirrels chatter,
Sharing secrets of cheesy patter.
They giggle at plans, oh so sly,
While birds burst forth with a cheeky cry.

A frog croaks jokes on a lily pad,
While rabbits laugh till they're quite mad.
Wise old tree with bark so worn,
Chimes in tales from yester morn.

The fireflies dance in flickering glee,
Lighting up stories, wild and free.
Every leaf a laughter-prone purse,
In this merry, buzzing universe.

Humor springs from roots and boughs,
Underneath the laughing cows.
Every shadow flutters with cheer,
In this whimsical forest, my dear.

The Treetop Tickle

The branches sway with a ticklish breeze,
As tittering twigs tease whistling trees.
A playful breeze sends hats a-flying,
While hidden critters giggle and sighing.

The parrot squawks a silly song,
Hopping along, it can't go wrong.
Snakes slither in with a wiggly smile,
Sharing stories, one goofy style.

Beneath the canopy, whispers abound,
As mushroom caps bounce to a funny sound.
Each rustling leaf joins in the jest,
Nature's laughter, at its very best.

The sunbeams pierce like a jester's light,
Creating shadows that dance in delight.
With every chuckle, the woods come alive,
In the treetop tickle, joy will thrive.

Forest Frolics

In the glen, the raccoons play,
Chasing tales of the silliest day.
Each tumble and roll, a giggling spree,
With antics that sway from tree to tree.

The owls hoot in a rhythm so neat,
Guiding the dance of their fluffy feet.
Pigeons prance with a hoppy flair,
While hedgehogs wear hats, quite rare.

A waltz of ants in a line so fine,
Carrying crumbs like treasures divine.
Each tiny step, a careful try,
Bursting forth with a tiny sigh.

Wind whispers loud with a chuckle or two,
As creatures join in the frolics anew.
In every nook, fun stories unfold,
And laughter grows, bright and bold.

The Whimsy of Woodlands

Underneath a sky so blue,
The woodlander sings, with a comedic view.
Fairies flit with a butterfly's grace,
In this world, laughter takes place.

Toadstools dance with hues so bright,
While light-hearted shadows take flight.
Caterpillars trade the silliest puns,
And wrap their jokes in webs like runs.

As night draws close, the moon beams giggle,
Painting the earth with a whimsical wiggle.
Critters gather in a merry band,
Tickling fun with a gentle hand.

Laughter echoes from tree to sheer space,
In the heart of the woods, find your place.
With each little chuckle, a memory stays,
In the whimsy of woodlands, joy always plays.

Fragrant Fancies of Fun

In the meadow, bright and clear,
Laughter bubbles, full of cheer.
Flowers dance in playful glee,
Whispering secrets, come and see!

Bouncing bees with silly hats,
Chasing after giggling rats.
Sunlight peeks through leafy thorns,
Tickled toes on grassy lawns.

Jolly clouds drift high above,
Frolics share a gentle shove.
Breezy whispers, playful prance,
Join the world in happy dance!

Frothy frolics find their way,
Chasing shadows in the fray.
Every chuckle, every grin,
Sparks a giggle deep within!

The Joyous Clearing Beneath the Trees

Where the branches twist and sway,
Jesters frolic, come and play.
Dancing feet on soft green ground,
Echoes of a joyful sound.

Squirrels scamper, play their jokes,
Chasing shadows, making folks.
With a bounce and silly spin,
Every heart is drawn right in.

Butterflies in silly flight,
Fluttering through the sunny light.
Under trees that laugh and sigh,
Whimsical dreams float by and by.

Frogs croak tunes, a comic choir,
While the breeze plays on the lyre.
In this clearing, time stands still,
Filled with joy, an endless thrill!

Dewdrops of Delight

Morning brings a sparkly glow,
Dewdrops hang on blades below.
Each a gem, a glistening tease,
Whispers laughter on the breeze.

Tiny bugs in bubble suits,
Skip along in merry hoots.
Nature's harmony in song,
Dancing where the giggles throng.

Hopscotch paths of sunlit beams,
In the midst of playful dreams.
Laughter echoes, bright and bold,
In the stories yet untold.

Raindrops fall like bouncing balls,
Creating splashes, joyful calls.
In this world of pure delight,
Every moment, magically bright!

Treetop Tickle Fest

Up in branches, high and wide,
Squirrels play as friends collide.
With a leap and cheeky grin,
Start the laughter, let it spin!

Tickled wings of passing birds,
Share their secrets, laugh like nerds.
Wiggly worms hold silly chats,
In their tiny, wriggly spats.

Sunshine spilling down like gold,
A tickle fight, the brave, the bold.
Branches sway and giggles soar,
Treetop antics, evermore.

With each plop and playful bounce,
Joy ignites and hearts denounce.
This fest of giggles finds its way,
To light our lives, come what may!

Chuckles Hidden in the Thicket

Amid the trees, a sound did creep,
A vintage joke, a secret keep.
With every rustle, laughter spills,
Beneath the boughs, the humor fills.

Squirrels giggle, birds take flight,
In this realm, all feels just right.
Ticklish roots and smiling stones,
Nature's jest, the joy it loans.

Giggling shadows dart and play,
As sunlight dances on the way.
Each little path, a tale to tell,
Of chuckles shared—oh, can you dwell?

With every breeze, a punchline comes,
Wit with the whispers, oh, how it drums!
In hidden corners, snickers bloom,
In thickets where we banish gloom.

Giggling Leaves

Leaves are chortling in the breeze,
In whispers soft, they tease with ease.
A tickle here, a jiggle there,
Every branch joins in the flair.

Sunshine sparkles, laughter clear,
A merry tune for all to hear.
With every rustle, joy takes flight,
As daisies dance, all feels so bright.

Mischief brews in every shade,
A jolly serenade displayed.
Beneath the boughs, the fun abounds,
In playful leaps, the laughter sounds.

Come join the merriment most grand,
Where chuckles spread across the land.
In giggling leaves, let spirits soar,
To celebrate the joy we adore!

Giggles Among the Branches

High above, the breezes wrap,
Nature chuckles, what a trap!
Winks and nudges through the trees,
In playful whispers, share the tease.

Branches sway with giddy cheer,
Guffaws echo far and near.
The critters join, a lively host,
In rib-tickling tales, they love the most.

Dappled sunbeams twinkle bright,
As shadows play in pure delight.
Each crack of wood, a joke so sweet,
In this woodland, laughter's treat.

So climb with giggles, up so high,
Feel the joy beneath the sky.
For in this place where humor thrives,
The spirit of fun, it truly strives!

Jolly Jests in the Wilderness

In wild retreats, the fun begins,
With jests that flap like playful fins.
The bushes hum a comic tune,
While rabbits dance beneath the moon.

Each twig a punchline, swift and sly,
Nature's sketches, we can't deny.
Caterpillars share their wit,
As giggles burst from every slit.

Here laughter quilts the forest floor,
In jolly jests, we can't ignore.
Squirrels gossip, owls roll their eyes,
Amidst the trees, the humor lies.

So gather 'round, let laughter ring,
With every jitter, hear us sing.
In wilds where joy and fun collide,
A world of jests, where smiles abide!

The Grove of Joyful Whispers

In a nook where shadows play,
Laughter dances, light and gay.
Ticklish leaves, a playful tease,
Whispers float upon the breeze.

Squirrels scamper, full of cheer,
Chasing laughter everywhere.
They juggle acorns, drop them too,
Giggles echo, skies so blue.

Sunbeams peek through branches wide,
Nature's giggles, can't abide.
Bouncing bunnies, hop on cue,
Each twist brings a joke for two.

At sunset, joy takes its flight,
The trees giggle, dimming light.
Under stars, the laughter grows,
In this realm, the fun just flows.

Frolic in the Forest

In the woods where the wild things clap,
Frogs wear crowns, take a nap.
Mice in tuxedos bow and sway,
To the rhythm of bright ballet.

Woodpeckers drum a silly beat,
While all the critters tap their feet.
A parade of ants, quite a sight,
Marching on, with pure delight.

Pinecones tumble down the hill,
Bursting laughter, what a thrill.
The happy trees join in the fun,
Their branches dance, each and one.

At twilight, shadows twirl and spin,
Creating smiles, can't help but grin.
In this forest, joy's the law,
Every step leaves you in awe.

Riddles in the Rustling Foliage

Leaves chatter with a mousy grin,
Whispered jokes, let the fun begin.
A riddle born from twigs and vines,
Answers hidden in gentle signs.

Caterpillars in bow ties wink,
As butterflies flit, cause us to think.
Each rustle tells a quirky tale,
Along the branches, winds set sail.

The trunk speaks in a playful tone,
While shadows mimic all alone.
Squirrels crack a nutty jest,
In the foliage, they jest the best.

Evening falls, a soft retreat,
Yet the laughter won't be beat.
In this bushy home, we'll stay,
Making fun our everyday.

The Joyful Boughs

Higher up where joy is found,
Trees wear laughter all around.
Boughs sway gently, tickle air,
Each soft giggle, a playful dare.

Chirping birds sing silly songs,
In their chorus, nothing's wrong.
Acorns roll with a tiny thud,
Nature's giggles turn to fun flood.

Underneath, the critters play,
Cartwheeling in the light of day.
Branches wave a cheerful hello,
While blossoms spin a joyous show.

As night descends, the glee remains,
With moonlight playing in the lanes.
In this bough of smiles and sighs,
The laughter twinkles in night skies.

Giggling Glimpses of Daylight

In the morning light, they play,
Chasing shadows, bright and gay.
Laughter spills like morning dew,
Tickling toes and skies so blue.

Silly squirrels in a dance,
Twist and tumble, what a chance.
Wiggly worms in tights so small,
Join the fun, they have a ball.

Bouncy bunnies hop about,
In the park, there is no doubt.
Chirping birds join in the spree,
Making music carefree and free.

As the sun begins to fade,
Sunbeams wink, a bright charade.
In the twilight, giggles grow,
Whispers soft, the moon's soft glow.

Folly Under the Foliage

Under leafy canopies,
Witty whispers float in breeze.
Jesters dance on grassy floor,
Round and round forevermore.

Giggling pebbles, silly stones,
Join the laughter, make new tones.
Bumblebees with buzzing cheer,
Buzz around, they've got no fear.

Mischief lurks in every nook,
Grab a friend and take a look.
Rustling leaves, a sudden scare,
Splitting sides with every dare.

Every giggle, every sigh,
Echoes softly, oh my, oh my!
Underneath, the world's aglow,
Where the joy resides, we know.

GiggleBough Bliss

On the branches, joy resides,
With the breeze, the laughter glides.
Bouncing boughs in sunlit cheer,
Whispers tickle, bringing near.

Chasing giggles, hearts so light,
Hopscotch lanes, what a sight!
Wobbly steps on leaf-rimmed trails,
Sail through life, on humor's sails.

Tickled by the sun's warm ray,
Catch the giggles, come what may.
Frolicking under skies so bright,
Life's a jest in pure delight.

Swaying gently, laughter flows,
Blooming joy in every rose.
Spreading smiles, a contagious bliss,
In the glade, you cannot miss.

Burst of Merriment

Laughter bubbles, pops and cracks,
In the breeze, it never lacks.
Bouncing balls on sunny days,
Skipping stones in giddy plays.

Chirpy crickets sing a tune,
Underneath the watchful moon.
Jolly frogs in little hats,
Join the dance with silly spats.

With a wink, the flowers chat,
Making jest of this and that.
Joyful prances, skip and hop,
Each new giggle makes you stop.

Every moment, bursting bright,
Life's a canvas colored light.
In the fields, let laughter reign,
In this bliss, we'll always gain.

Playful Spirits of the Pines

In a forest where shadows play,
Squirrels chatter and dance all day.
The branches sway with a giggle or two,
As the breeze whispers secrets, just for you.

A rabbit hops with a twist and twirl,
While flowers nod, making petals whirl.
The sun peeks in, a cheeky grin wide,
Inviting all critters to laugh and slide.

A feathered friend sings a silly song,
While the ants march in a parade strong.
Every step brings a chuckle anew,
In this realm where joy is the cue.

At dusk, the fireflies join the fun,
Dancing like stars till the day is done.
With every flicker, a laugh takes flight,
In this playful world of sheer delight.

Laughter's Leafy Abode

Amidst the trees where the giggles reside,
The mischief-makers take joy in their stride.
A monkey swings with a cheeky little wave,
While the mushrooms chuckle, so bold and brave.

The brook babbles jokes, waters sparkle bright,
Each ripple a smile, a gleeful sight.
A turtle in sunglasses moves slow and sly,
While the butterflies giggle, drifting nearby.

As shadows lengthen, the stories unfold,
A coyote tells tales, a bit too bold.
With rustles and chuckles, the company grows,
In this leafy abode where laughter flows.

The stars peek down, their twinkle a tease,
While the owls hoot softly, dancing with ease.
In this whimsical haven, joy's in the air,
Every leaf carries laughter, everywhere!

Woodland Whimsy

A hedgehog prances, a joyful little soul,
With acorns scattered, he plays the role.
Frogs leap and croak in a merry choir,
Each splash in the pond ignites a desire.

The mushrooms wear hats in curious styles,
Embarking on adventures that stretch for miles.
A wise old owl with glasses so round,
Shares tales of humor that resound.

Little creatures gather, their giggles collide,
In twinkling light where pure joy resides.
A dance of the fireflies, a magical sight,
As the moon joins in, bathing all in light.

The whispering breeze adds its own little tune,
As laughter and whimsy make all hearts swoon.
In this woodland wonder, so cheerful and free,
Every moment's a joke, a giggle, a spree!

The Dance of the Delighted

Beneath the trees where the vines intertwine,
The critters all gather, their faces divine.
A raccoon spins tales with a wink and a grin,
While the daisies sway, inviting the spin.

From snickers of rabbits, a chorus ensues,
With foxes that jive, in psychedelic shoes.
Each leap and bounds ignites the whole place,
In a wondrous display, full of joy and grace.

As twilight descends, the revelry grows,
With giggles and shouts that nobody knows.
The breeze carries laughter, sweet as a song,
In the heart of the forest, where we all belong.

So join in the dance, let your spirits ignite,
As the night wraps around, a beautiful sight.
In the realm of delight, where laughs are the key,
Every heart gets to twirl, wild and free!

Playful Shadows Among the Leaves

In the dance of light and shade,
Whispers of laughter cascade.
Squirrels juggle acorns wide,
While giggling breezes chide.

Frogs croak jokes with such delight,
Caterpillars laugh in flight.
Dancing under the twinkling sun,
Every leaf smiles, every run.

Puppies chase their own wagging tails,
Bouncing 'round like wacky gales.
Caught in the thrill of the game,
Nature's chuckles are never tame.

With each rustle, a guffaw near,
Joy hops close, drawing near.
Amidst the trees, so bold and bright,
Playful shadows keep guests light.

Merry Melodies of Mischief

Wind whirls tunes of snap and crack,
Birds chirp sweetly, never lack.
A frolicsome fox in a hat,
Jumps around, a singing brat.

In the brush, the crickets play,
Humming mischief night and day.
Butterflies twirl in silly reels,
Giggling gently at their heels.

Jays in a chorus, bold and clear,
Singing the truth you want to hear.
Every branch holds a playful jest,
Nature's laughter is simply the best.

Twirling leaves join the feast,
Nuts and berries, a little beast.
Merry melodies float through the air,
Heartfelt giggles everywhere.

Chortles Beneath the Canopy

Beneath the green, oh what a sight,
Creatures laughing, feeling light.
A rabbit slips in a puddle sly,
Hopping back with a gleam in eye.

The trees sway in a funny dance,
Inviting all to join the chance.
Bumbles buzz and tickle ears,
Nature's jest brings forth the cheers.

Chubby owls on branches low,
Swapping tales of friends in tow.
Each flapping wing sings a rhyme,
The joy of now, the bliss of time.

Every leaf teems with a giggle,
As shadows weave in playful wiggle.
In this joy, we find our glee,
A world wrapped in hilarity.

Sunlit Snickers and Sprightly Sighs

As sunlight pours, a warming glow,
The world awakens, ready to show.
Bouncy critters in a stretchy pose,
Tickle the grass, where silliness flows.

Frolicsome children run with glee,
Twirling hats in the gentle breeze.
The old oak chuckles at their play,
Waving branches in a cheeky sway.

The brook giggles, bubbling bright,
Echoing tales of pure delight.
Each ripple whispers, sweet and clear,
A serenade for all to hear.

Sunlit snickers blend with sighs,
As clouds drift by in fun disguise.
All around, merriment rings,
In this realm where laughter springs.

Chuckling Through the Dappled Light

In the sunlight, shadows play,
Laughter dances, bright and gay.
A squirrel slips, a branch does sway,
Nature's jest on display.

A butterfly, with wings so bold,
Flits around with tales untold.
The flowers giggle, colors unfold,
In this light, joy's pure gold.

The whispers of the breeze are sly,
Tickling leaves as they flutter by.
Even the rocks seem to comply,
Cracking jokes that make us sigh.

As day wears on, the fun won't cease,
Every rustle brings sweet release.
Here where laughter finds its peace,
In dappled light, our worries decrease.

The Jolly Jubilee

In fields of cheer, the dancers twirl,
A merry band of laughing girls.
With every spin, the joy unfurls,
As sunlight on the daisies swirls.

A rabbit hops with flair and style,
He's wearing pants, it makes us smile.
The playful leaves join in the pile,
Nature's party goes a while.

The birds above sing silly tunes,
While frogs below do funny croons.
Each rustling leaf in afternoon,
Chimes in with a happy boon.

With pie and cakes, the feast is grand,
Beneath a bright and cheerful band.
Join us here, take a joyful stand,
In this silly, splendid land.

Nonsense in the Nature

Why did the tree wear a hat today?
To catch the rain that loved to play!
A babbling brook, in bright display,
Tickles the stones with its ballet.

A hedgehog slips on a rubber shoe,
With tiny shoes, he skips right through.
The flowers giggle in every hue,
A sight so strange, a funny view!

Clouds smile down with fluffy faces,
As squirrels run through endless races.
Mirth is found in all the places,
Nature's joy in funny traces.

In this dance, reality bends,
Where whimsy spreads, and laughter blends.
Join the fun, as nonsense sends,
A message that joy never ends.

Playful Echoes of the Earth

The wind whispers secrets, cheeky and bright,
 While giggles bounce in pure delight.
A chipmunk's chuckle, a comical sight,
 In this realm of mischief, all feels right.

The grass sighs softly, ticklish and green,
 Under the sun's affectionate sheen.
With each little joke, the hills convene,
 A rollicking world, a joyful scene.

Bees hum melodies, silly and sweet,
 With wiggly dances, they skip, then repeat.
Nature performs in a whimsy feat,
 A joyful jest no one can beat.

As shadows stretch and day turns to night,
Stars giggle softly, twinkling with might.
In this playful echo, everything's bright,
Where laughter is magic, and hearts take flight.

Delightful Dappled Dreams

In a patch of sunlit cheer,
Where shadows dance and prance,
A squirrel juggles acorns near,
While flowers sway and glance.

A rabbit slips on dewy grass,
With a giggle, hops away,
A butterfly—a fancy lass,
Twirls bright in grand display.

Chirping birds in silly fight,
Chase a worm with cheerful glee,
They tumble down in pure delight,
And shout as loud as can be.

While breezes tease the leafy trees,
A chorus of chuckles follows,
Their laughter floats on playful breeze,
As joy within us swallows.

The Lightness of Laughter

Bouncing beams of sunny rays,
Toadstools wear a giggly hat,
A mole performs in odd ballet,
While crickets hum, 'Imagine that!'

The breeze throws whispers, soft and sly,
As clouds parade in cotton shapes,
A duck attempts a daring fly,
And lands among the grape escapes.

With each good-natured prank revealed,
The daisies giggle, stretch their heads,
In laughter's arms, the world is healed,
Where every dreamer lightens treads.

Oh, gentle scenes of wild and free,
Painted in hues of joy so bright,
A symphony of comedy,
Where hearts release and take to flight.

Nature's Comic Con

In the wild, where jesters roam,
A frog in tights will leap and croak,
He's king of laughs in leafy dome,
As spiteful squirrels burst with joke.

A hedgehog wears a spiky crown,
He tells tall tales of daring feats,
While woeful owls, in gowns, sit down,
Their wise remarks bring playful beats.

Frisky foxes swirl and spin,
With tails like ribbons in the air,
They tumble forth with mischievous grin,
As laughter threads through every hair.

The fields host laughter—grand and loud,
A circus bright, with joy on show,
Where nature loves to take a bow,
Delightful humor steals the flow.

The Whirl of Whimsy

In the glen where giggles twine,
A gopher cartwheels in the sun,
With sparkly dust, he draws a line,
And all the critters take their run.

A shifty badger plays a prank,
He hides behind a leafy bush,
Then jumps out with a playful thank,
As rabbits pause, then start to rush.

With each frolic, laughter swells,
The daisies nod as if they know,
In harmony, the rhythm dwells,
The world's a stage, a comical show.

So join the dance, don't hesitate,
In nature's dance of merry spins,
Together, we will celebrate,
The whimsy where all joy begins.

The Secret Garden of Grins

In a place where laughter blooms,
Tickling toes and cheerful tunes,
Silly squirrels dance on the grass,
Echoes of joy as hours pass.

Whispers of secrets in the air,
Giggling flowers everywhere,
Bouncing bees in a joyful race,
Hilarious hues in every space.

Marigolds wear a playful grin,
Chasing shadows, let the fun begin,
Chirpy birds sing in delight,
As the sun sets, a happy sight.

The shrubs sway with a comic sway,
In this garden where joys play,
Every corner holds a surprise,
A chuckle hidden, oh what a prize!

Joyful Rustles in the Underbrush

Beneath the leaves where the giggles hide,
Rascally rabbits hop with pride,
Bubbles of laughter in the air,
Every rustle makes you stop and stare.

Whiskers twitch with a cheeky tease,
The critters dance in sketchy ease,
Sunlight filters through the trees,
Making shadows that shimmy and sneeze.

Crickets chirp a merry tune,
While butterflies spin a funny swoon,
Furry friends roll on the ground,
In this place of joy, fun is found.

With every step, a giggle pops,
As silly squirrels hang from the tops,
Laughter bubbles, never a rush,
In this underbrush, happiness crush.

Frolicsome Ferns and Fancies

Frolicsome ferns sway with flair,
Dancing breezes tickle your hair,
In every shade, a story told,
With chuckles of green, bright and bold.

Curious critters peek and prance,
In the light of their merry dance,
Jolly pumpkins, round and bright,
Laughing shadows, what a sight!

Underneath the playful skies,
With smiling bugs of all sizes,
Pattering paws in glee collide,
As nature's fun cannot hide.

Amidst the ferns, giggles soar,
A whimsical world, forevermore,
Where every leaf holds a cheer,
And smiles grow bright from ear to ear.

Giggles in the Grove of Dreams

In a grove where giggles reign,
Wondrous visions, never plain,
Dreamy daisies winking bright,
With each chuckle, hearts take flight.

Bouncing beds of mossy cream,
Whispers swirl, like a sweet dream,
Playful shadows leap and glide,
A tapestry of joy, wide.

Lunar moths flutter with glee,
Splendid sights for all to see,
Nonsense stories flip and flop,
As friendly fungi never stop.

In this grove where laughter thrives,
Every heartbeat joyfully dives,
With whimsical whispers in the breeze,
Where happiness grows among the trees.

Ticklish Tendrils

In a sunny nook, where shadows play,
Whispers of joy dance light and gay.
Branches shake with chortles bright,
Swaying gently, pure delight.

Squirrels giggle, tossing nuts,
While rabbits' antics leave us in juts.
Breezes tease with a flowing tickle,
As laughter bounces, a merry trickle.

Leaves flutter soft, like hands at cheer,
Every rustle brings laughter near.
Roots wiggle with glee, oh what a sight,
In this wild spot, hearts take flight.

Echoes of chuckles reveal the charms,
Nature's humor, a world that warms.
Here in our laughter, we're never alone,
In the ticklish arms of the unknown.

The Allure of Laughter

Under the sun's warm, golden rays,
Lies a land where everyone plays.
Jokes hang like fruit on lush green trees,
Tickling noses with the softest breeze.

Puppies prance with clumsy grace,
While kittens tumble in a fluffy race.
Frogs in hats, what a quirky sight,
All join in the giggling delight.

Across the meadows, squeals of fun,
Chasing shadows, we all can run.
Butterflies flutter in laughter's flight,
As joy twinkles in the softest light.

Here every chuckle is a fresh breeze,
Spreading joy among the towering trees.
Within this realm, our spirits soar,
Wrapped in laughter forevermore.

Cackles in the Clearing

In the heart of the wild, where mischief thrives,
Lies a secret space where giggle survives.
Bouncing bubbles of chuckles burst,
In this merry spot, we're all well-versed.

Woodpeckers tap in a silly beat,
While rabbits gather for a tasty treat.
Chirping birds join in the fun,
Mirth and joy can't be outdone.

Mushrooms wear caps like tiny hats,
Crickets chorus alongside spats.
Silly shadows waltz on the green,
Celebrating laughter, a joyous scene.

In this clearing, worries erase,
With every snicker, we find our place.
A world of giggles, no need for fear,
In this enchanted space, we cheer.

Sprites and Silliness

Amidst the ferns where pixies play,
Laughter lights up the gloomiest day.
Whimsy wanders on fluttering wings,
Sprouting hilarity, oh the joy it brings!

With every flicker of tiny lights,
Comes a chorus of giggles, shining bright.
Goblins trip on their own two feet,
Turning antics into a merry feat.

Mirthful echoes fill the air,
As friends gather round for the silliest dare.
Spinning and dancing in whimsical haste,
In this land of laughter, we're never misplaced.

So join the sprites in their playful schemes,
Where smiles abound and laughter beams.
In this merry realm, let worries cease,
And bask in the joy, the sweetest peace.

Delightful Echoes of the Forest Floor

In the shade where whispers play,
Squirrels dance with glee all day.
Leaves giggle as they tumble down,
Nature's jesters wear a crown.

Butterflies prance, no shoes required,
The air is filled, laughter inspired.
Rabbits hop with cheeky flair,
Every creak returns a dare.

Mushrooms wobble in silly rows,
Tickled by breezes, how it flows!
Beneath the boughs, joy takes flight,
Echoes of fun, pure delight!

Leaves poke fun, rustling in jest,
In this place, everyone feels blessed.
Nature chuckles, so light and free,
Join the fun, come laugh with me!

The Lively Loss of Seriousness

Hats made of daisies, worn askew,
A turtle laughs as it passes through.
With each wiggle, a giggle grows,
Chasing seriousness, off it goes.

A fluttering kite, a silly sight,
Caught in a tree, a friendly fight.
The clouds above start to chuckle too,
Dropping down raindrops, just for you!

With every hop and skip we make,
Laughter ripples like a lake.
In this realm of joy's embrace,
Lively hearts find their place.

So shed your weight, come play along,
The world's a stage; join in the song!
For chasing woes is quite the art,
In this joyful dance, we'll never part.

Unruly Joys in the Leafy Orbit

In the swirl of leaves, chaos reigns,
Each step a giggle, laughing pains.
Frogs wear hats, so very odd,
These merry creatures, a playful nod.

The wind plays tricks, a playful tease,
Rustling branches, shaking knees.
A hedgehog rolls, soft and round,
In this revelry, joy is found.

Acorns tumble in a game of chase,
Come join the fun, it's a lively space!
Every twirl, a carol sung,
Leafy orbits, forever young!

With each burst of laughter, spirits soar,
Nature's jests, we can't ignore.
In the wild, where smiles align,
Unruly joys, the stars will shine!

The Cheerful Canopy Concert

Beneath the branches, a chorus sings,
With every note, hilarity clings.
Crickets chirp in sync and style,
Creating laughter, mile by mile.

The sunbeams dance through leafy holes,
Warming up all the joyful souls.
An owl hoots in a funny way,
Leading the jokes of the play today!

Each little creature joins the band,
A symphony in this leafy land.
With giddy tones, the forest sways,
In the concert of life, joy displays.

So raise your voice, let laughter ring,
In this celebration, we're all kings.
Under the canopy's funny shade,
Join the merriment that we've made!

The Playful Pathways

Beneath the bright and sunny skies,
The rabbits hop with joyful cries.
Squirrels twirl in merry dance,
While daisies sway in a silly prance.

A frog sings tunes on a lilypad throne,
While turtles giggle, never alone.
The path is paved with laughter's sound,
Where every step brings joy around.

Butterflies flutter in a dizzy spin,
Tickling flowers, a whimsical win.
The air is sweet with jokes and grins,
As chuckles echo, where fun begins.

Join the parade of silly delight,
In every corner, smiles ignite.
For on this path of jest and cheer,
Every moment's filled with laughter near.

Laughter in the Meadow

In fields where daisies bloom so wide,
The giggles of children can't be denied.
A puppy chases his own wild tail,
While butterflies whisper secrets frail.

The wind carries tricks on its playful breeze,
As grasshoppers jump with effortless ease.
Sunshine glistens on dew-drops bright,
Each chuckle dances, pure delight.

Come find the gnomes in mismatched hats,
Who tell silly stories about their chitchats.
Their laughter rings, a melodic cheer,
In the meadow's heart, fun draws near.

A picnic spread with goodies galore,
Every bite accompanied by laughter's roar.
As twilight falls, fireflies glow,
The meadow buzzes with joy in tow.

Mischief Under the Maple

Beneath the branches, secrets sway,
Where squirrels plan their silly play.
With acorns tossed and pranks unfurled,
Their laughter echoes through the world.

A raccoon dons a mask for style,
Stealing snacks with a cheeky smile.
The leaves giggle as they shimmer bright,
In the soft embrace of the fading light.

Children creep with hands on their hats,
Trying to catch the playful sprats.
But mischief hides in every nook,
With whispers soft like a storybook.

As shadows grow and night draws near,
The giggles rise in the warm atmosphere.
Under the maple, fun never sleeps,
In the laughter's depth, the memory keeps.

The Chorus of the Cheery

In the forest, a joyous choir sings,
With frogs croaking, and birdies on swings.
Each note a chuckle, each line a jest,
In this cheerful nook where laughter rests.

The owls hoot in a whimsical tune,
While critters gather, beneath the moon.
Their antics wrapped in night's embrace,
Creating giggles that never erase.

A hedgehog jigs with a skip and a hop,
While raccoons dance, they never stop.
The moonbeams twirl with a playful glee,
Joining the fun, oh what a spree!

From leaves that rustle to stars that blink,
The chorus of laughter, the joy in sync.
Together they sway, in nature's grand show,
Celebrating the joy in every glow.

Silly Serenades Under Stars

Under a moonlit glow,
The frogs are putting on a show.
With top hats and a cane,
They waltz without a grain.

Squirrels dance in the breeze,
Tickling each other with ease.
A raccoon joins the fun,
He juggles nuts one by one.

Laughter rings in the night,
As fireflies twinkle bright.
Each giggle, a delight,
Fluffy clouds drift in flight.

The stars sing out a tune,
While crickets keep in swoon.
Nature's jesters in line,
In silly tunes, they shine.

Haikus of Hijinks

Grasshopper steals snacks,
Juggling berries on his back—
Joyful leaps and cracks.

Cats plotting a prank,
Piles of yarn all in rank,
Twist and twirl and clank.

Chirpy birds conspire,
To sing songs that inspire,
In harmony, they wire.

Tangled in the trees,
Whispers carried by the breeze,
Laughter floats with ease.

Twinkling Treetops

Above branches spin tales,
With giggling leaves, they sail.
The breeze plays a flute,
While napping owls hoot.

Silly shadows prance,
Chasing each other in a dance.
Twinkling lights peek out,
What's this all about?

A chattering parade,
Squirrels dressed in charade.
With acorns in tow,
They put on quite a show.

Hoots echo in glee,
Under the joyful tree.
Nature's jesters rise,
In this realm of the wise.

Jests Among the Ivy

Ivy climbs up high,
Making a home for a guy.
A snail with a hat,
And a petting cat.

Mice in tiny suits,
Hosting grand card disputes.
With cheese for a stake,
They strategize and break.

Laughter echoes near,
As the hedgehogs cheer.
With tiny flags in hand,
They form a little band.

Creeping up the wall,
Wonders at their hall.
Nature's jesters thrive,
In the jests, they're alive.

Sprightly Shadows

Among the trees, the whispers play,
Silly shadows dance today.
Bouncing, twirling, with a glee,
Chasing laughter, wild and free.

A squirrel hops, a bird takes flight,
Jokesters winking in the light.
Leaves rustle with a giggle sound,
In this merry, leafy ground.

The sunbeams spray like silly string,
Nature hums, and frogs do sing.
Beneath the boughs, hilarity blooms,
In this place, joy always zooms.

So join the games where spirits soar,
In a world of chuckles, and so much more.
With every step, a punniest cheer,
Sprightly shadows bring us near.

Frogs and Folly

In the pond where jesters play,
Frogs are jumping—hip hooray!
Warty faces, big and bright,
Hopping high in sheer delight.

They croak of jokes that lead us wrong,
Singing silly, ribbiting song.
Splashes echo like gabbling glee,
Folly reigns in every spree.

Skipping stones with playful flair,
Outside the norm, without a care.
One little leap, a splash, then qui-
The laughter keeps on soaring high!

At dusk they toast the sun's retreat,
In bubbly joy, their hearts repeat.
For in their world of muck and mirth,
Frogs tell tales of happy girth.

Nature's Jesting Heart

Under canopy, chaos reigns,
The trees chuckle, laughter gains.
The flowers wink, their colors bright,
Whispering secrets, sheer delight.

Buzzing bees in goofy flight,
Dance around—a funny sight!
They stumble, drop their nectar sweet,
Nature's jesters, skipping beat.

A hedgehog rolls, a tumble here,
With each somersault, we cheer!
In every rustle, fun we find,
Jesting heart is nature's kind.

As clouds giggle, drift and sway,
In every hue, the whimsy stays.
Life's a circus in this park,
Where joys are sharp but never stark.

The Laughter that Blooms

In the garden where spirits play,
Blooming laughter paints the day.
Petal whispers and giggle puffs,
Tickle the air, oh so soft, so tough.

Here a daisy, there a joke,
Wobbly stems, and laughter spoke.
Sunshine grins, the sky's a clown,
Painting smiles across the town.

Ladybugs dance, in dots so bright,
Jovial moves, what a sight!
Every bloom, a love to share,
In laughter's arms, we all take care.

So come, dear friend, let's celebrate,
In the garden where we can't wait.
For every flower's upward glance,
Sprouts a giggle, luring us to dance.

The Harlequin Hideaway

In a nook where chuckles grow,
The jester dances to and fro.
With every twist and silly leap,
The laughter lingers, oh so deep.

Beneath a roof of painted glee,
They sing of joy, wild and free.
A juggling clown, a pie in flight,
Turns mundane days to sheer delight.

Squeaky shoes on cobbled stone,
Each step a quirk, a joyful tone.
With every giggle, spirits soar,
Within this hideaway galore.

So come and join this merry play,
Where every heart finds room to sway.
In painted realms of pure surprise,
The jester's jest never dies!

Jocular Journeys in the Sierra

Through mountain trails where laughter rings,
A wobbly goat on silly springs.
Chasing shadows, playing hide,
While giggling echoes bounce and glide.

In picnics bright with pies in tow,
A skit unfolds with each new show.
The squirrels tease with cheeky flair,
As friends break bread without a care.

On every peak, the humor clears,
The grumpy clouds yield to no fears.
So let the chuckles fill the air,
And ticklish breezes tousle hair.

With each step up, the heartbeats race,
As chuckles spark, our worries erase.
Amongst the pines, we roam and play,
In jocular tunes, we pass the day.

Dances of Delightful Spirits

Beneath the moon, the sprites do twirl,
With wild capers, they spin and whirl.
Their laughter weaves through misty night,
In joyous leaps, a wondrous sight.

With stepping stones of marshmallow dreams,
They bounce on air like flowing streams.
Each giggle forms a starry spark,
As mischief plays in the moonlit dark.

They dip and dive in rainbow hues,
In silly hats and oversized shoes.
With every twist, their charm ignites,
Igniting joy in hearts and sights.

So join the dance, don't hesitate,
In this world of fun, it's never late.
With spirits bright and laughter clear,
The night is ours, let's hold it dear!

Whimsical Whispers of the Wind

The gentle breeze sings soft and sweet,
Whispering secrets with playful feet.
Each gust brings chuckles from afar,
As it tickles trees and plays guitar.

It twirls the leaves in joyous flight,
Encouraging squirrels to take up fright.
While giggles settle on blooming flowers,
Transforming minutes into hours.

The wind plays tricks on floppy hats,
Stealing them from busy chats.
With every swipe, a hearty laugh,
A dance of glee, a lightened path.

In this realm of whimsy and cheer,
The whispers beckon, come draw near.
For in the air, and under skies,
Laughter reigns as joy complies!

Laughter's Lush Retreat

Beneath the trees where laughter flows,
Silly squirrels wear funny clothes.
A bunny hops and trips with glee,
While giggles dance beneath the tree.

Chasing shadows, jokes take flight,
Bright butterflies flirt in the light.
Ticklish grass and ticklish toes,
Here, every chuckle freely grows.

Friendly frogs with jokes galore,
Croak out tales that we adore.
With each snicker, hearts grow light,
In this realm, it's pure delight.

Come join the fun, the joy, the cheer,
With every smile, the world is clear.
In this place where laughter's spread,
All worries vanish, joy is bred.

Whispers of Joyful Breezes

The breeze carries whispers, soft and bright,
As playful shadows dash in delight.
A dancing leaf, it twirls with grace,
Mischief sparkles on every face.

Tickling the flowers, the wind has fun,
As every petal kisses the sun.
A chirpy bird tells tales so wacky,
In this land, everything's a bit tacky.

Butterfingers drop their faves,
Silly antics that joyfully braves.
The sun's warm glow, a hug from above,
Wraps us tightly in laughter and love.

So let's dance with joy on this merry path,
Share our giggles, embrace the laugh.
In every corner, in every breeze,
Life's a comedy, with endless tease.

The Enchanted Meadow of Mirth

In a meadow where laughter sings,
The daisies wear their brightest rings.
Silly rabbits, they hop and play,
Chasing dreams throughout the day.

A jolly breeze tickles the grass,
Watch the clouds come and go as they pass.
Frolicking friends in a jovial race,
With silly smirks and a cheerful face.

The sunbeams dance on petals wide,
While tittering leaves join in for a ride.
A sudden splash—a puddle's call,
Every jump brings joy to all.

Under the sky, a light-hearted space,
Each giggling whisper falls into place.
So join the fun, let joy unfold,
In this enchanted land, let laughter be bold.

Echoes of Laughter in the Glen

Hidden away in a vibrant glen,
Where laughter lingers again and again.
The jolly fox, with tricks to share,
Spreads giggles and smiles, light as air.

With a wink and a nod from a wise old owl,
The antics of critters make everyone howl.
In every rustle, a new joke is born,
As merriment flutters with every dawn.

The brook bubbles softly, trailing along,
Its gurgling whispers join in the song.
Children's laughter can travel for miles,
While every turn brings new joyful smiles.

In this glen where fun takes its stand,
All friends unite, hand in hand.
With echoes of laughter that never tire,
In this magical place, joy does inspire.

The Laughter-Filled Dell

In a dell where laughter thrives,
Bouncing like the bees that dive.
Silly frogs in hats parade,
Tickling leaves in light cascade.

Squirrels giggle, tails in flight,
Jumping high, a comical sight.
Jokes whispered to the trees,
Rustling leaves like playful tease.

A babbling brook joins the fun,
Giggling softly in the sun.
Dance of shadows makes them grin,
Nature's humor wraps them in.

So come and join this merry spree,
In the dell, so wild and free.
Every chuckle fills the space,
Find joy in every little place.

Whimsy Beneath the Whirling Branches

Beneath branches that twist and sway,
A party of shadows comes out to play.
With playful twirls and a skip of feet,
The world becomes one big funny treat.

Chirping birds add to the tale,
Their songs are jokes that never fail.
Bunnies hop with a bounce and cheer,
In this funny land, there's no fear.

Leaves twirl down like confetti bright,
Spreading joy, oh what a sight!
Every creature wears a grin,
With a chuckle shared, we're all akin.

The sky bursts forth with hues that tease,
Colorful antics dance in the breeze.
Whirling like tops, we laugh and spin,
In whimsical wonder, let the fun begin.

Charm of the Chuckling Coves

In secret coves where chuckles play,
Every pebble shares a laugh today.
Waves that giggle on the shore,
Tumble in with a joyful roar.

Seashells giggle, secrets told,
Stories of mischief, brave and bold.
Sandcastles sport a smling crown,
While little crabs scuttle around.

The sun winks bright, a cheeky tease,
Catching rays with whims like these.
In every nook, a joke is spun,
Turning the tides of playful fun.

So join the dance of the happy scene,
In these coves, where we all convene.
With laughter echoing all around,
Joy spills forth from tiny mounds.

Jests Among the Jasmine

In a patch of jasmine sweetly blooms,
Laughter fills the air, dispelling glooms.
Buzzy bees in bow ties hum,
Roving lightly, here they come!

A butterfly flutters, tickling the nose,
With every landing, joy just grows.
Petals whisper giggles soft,
Inviting all to lift aloft.

The air is thick with jests and fun,
Bouncing laughter, no need to run.
Every breeze a playful poke,
Nature's comedy, a timeless joke.

So gather near this fragrant place,
With smiles that bloom, let's embrace.
When jasmine blooms, laughter flows,
In this magic, happiness grows.

www.ingramcontent.com/pod-product-compliance
Lightning Source LLC
Chambersburg PA
CBHW051648160426
43209CB00004B/843